LITTLE RED BOOK OF HOLIDAY QUOTES & TOASTS

Warm-hearted, Funny, & Entertaining Sayings for the Holidays

Team Golfwell

www.TeamGolfwell.com

Published by: Pacific Trust Holdings NZ Ltd., 2018

Contents

"It is, indeed, the season of regenerated feeling - the season for kindling, not merely the fire of hospitality in the hall, but the genial flame of charity in the heart." *- Washington Irving (1783 – 1859) American Writer*

Introduction

Theologian John Piper said reading sentences (rather than books) can be one of the most meaningful experiences in your life:

"What I have learned from about twenty years of serious reading is this: It is sentences that change my life, not books.

"What changes my life is some new glimpse of truth, some powerful challenge, some resolution to a long-standing dilemma, and these usually come concentrated in a sentence or two.

"I do not remember 99% of what I read, but if the 1% of each book or article I do remember is a life-changing insight, then I don't begrudge the 99%." *– John Piper, "Quantitative Hopelessness and the Immeasurable Moment"*

We hope you find these quotes & toasts humorous, entertaining and thought-provoking. We hope you use it for a reference for many Holiday gatherings or any family or friends' gatherings any time of the year.

We extend to all our readers our best wishes for an enjoyable and very happy Holiday Season!

Holiday Quotes & Toasts

"In the old days, it was not called the Holiday Season; the Christians called it 'Christmas' and went to church; the Jews called it 'Hanukkah' and went to synagogue; the atheists went to parties and drank. People passing each other on the street would say 'Merry Christmas!' or 'Happy Hanukkah!' or (to the atheists) 'Look out for the wall!" *- Dave Barry, Author and nationally syndicated humor columnist for the Miami Herald*

"Christmas is a bridge. We need bridges as the river of time flows past. Today's Christmas should mean creating happy hours for tomorrow and reliving those of yesterday."
- Gladys Taber, (1899–1980), Author and columnist for Ladies' Home Journal and Family Circle

"When we recall Christmas past, we usually find the simplest things - not the great occasions -

give off the greatest glow of happiness." *- Bob Hope (1903 - 2003) American comedian*

"If your Birthday is on Christmas day and you're not Jesus, you should start telling people your birthday is on June 9 or something. Just read up on the traits of a Gemini. Suddenly you're a multitasker who loves the color yellow.

"Because not only do you get stuck with them combo gift, you get the combo song. 'We wish you a merry Christmas - and happy birthday, Terry - we wish you a merry Christmas - happy birthday, Terry - we wish you a merry Christmas and a happy New Ye… Birthday, Terry!'" *- Ellen DeGeneres, American comedian, television host, actress, writer, and producer.*

Holiday Toast: "May you have the gladness of Christmas which is hope;

The spirit of Christmas which is peace;

The heart of Christmas which is love." *- Anon*

"'I don't know what to do!' cried Scrooge, laughing and crying in the same breath; and making a perfect Laocoön of himself with his stockings.

"'I am as light as a feather, I am as happy as an angel, I am as merry as a school-boy. I am as giddy as a drunken man. A merry Christmas to every-body! A happy New Year to all the world! Hallo here! Whoop! Hallo!'" *- Charles Dickens, (1812 - 1870) English Author from "A Christmas Carol"*

"Wisdom of the Ages: The Nativity. The Son of God was born in a manger - not surprising, have you seen the prices of hotel rooms in Bethlehem? Oy Vay! Merry Christmas, Happy Hanukkah, Peace!" *- Matthew D. Heines, Author, Deceptions of the Ages: "Mormons" Freemasons and Extraterrestrials*

Carolers: "We wish you a merry Christmas" is the most demanding song ever. It starts off all nice and a second later you have an angry mob at your door scream-singing, 'Now bring us some figgy pudding and bring it RIGHT HERE. WE WON'T GO UNTIL WE GET SOME SO BRING IT RIGHT HERE.'

"Also, they're rhyming 'here' with 'here.' That's just sloppy. I'm not rewarding unrequested, lazy singers with their aggressive pudding demands. There should be a remix of that song that homeowners can sing that's all 'I didn't even ask for your sh*tty song, you filthy beggars. I've called the cops. Who is this even working on? Has anyone you've tried this on actually given you pudding? Fig-flavored pudding? Is that even a thing?' It doesn't rhyme but it's not like they're trying either.

"And then the carolers would be like, 'SO BRING US SOME GIN AND TONIC AND LET'S HAVE A BEER,' and then I'd be like, 'Well, I guess that's more reasonable. Fine. You can come in for one drink.'

"Technically that would be a good way to get free booze. Like trick-or-treat but for singy alcoholics. Oh my God, I finally understand caroling." *- Jenny Lawson, Author, "Furiously Happy: A Funny Book About Horrible Things"*

Holiday Toast: "May you be poor in misfortune this Christmas,

And rich in blessings,

Slow to make enemies,

Quick to make friends,

And rich or poor, slow or quick,

As happy as the New Year is long."

- Old Irish Toast

"Heap on more wood! - the wind is chill;

But let it whistle as it will,

We'll keep our Christmas merry still."

- Sir Walter Scott (1771 - 1832) Novelist

"One can never have enough socks," said Dumbledore. "Another Christmas has come and gone, and I didn't get a single pair. People will

insist on giving me books.” *- J.K. Rowling, Author, “Harry Potter and the Sorcerer's Stone”*

“I wrapped my Christmas presents early this year, but I used the wrong paper. See, the paper I used said 'Happy Birthday' on it.

“I didn't want to waste it, so I just wrote 'Jesus' on it.” *- Demetri Martin, Comedian*

“We try to make the name longer and longer every year. First, it was 'Larry the Cable Guy's Christmas Spectacular.'

“Then it was 'It's a Very Larry Christmas.'

“Now it's 'Larry the Cable Guy's Hula-palooza Christmas Luau.'

“I'll tell you what it is: It's funny. That's what it is. Who cares what the name of it is? It is a funny special.” *- Larry the Cable Guy, American Comedian*

“My mom and dad always tried to make Christmas special for us. We were poor, but it's

funny because we had no idea." *- Johnny Mathis, American singer*

"I keep saying this - and I keep putting it off because I get busy - but I keep saying one year I'm gonna tape our Thanksgiving dinner or, like, our Christmas dinner and maybe put it on my website just for people to see how funny it really is, how much fun it really, really is." *- Tony Rock, Comedian*

"The main reason Santa is so jolly is because he knows where all the bad girls live." *- George Carlin (1937 – 2008) Comedian*

"Christmas in the Buckley household is hilarious - at the family dinner, we all have to do a song, no matter if you can sing in tune." *- Jessie Buckley, Irish singer and actress*

"And the Grinch, with his Grinch-feet ice cold in the snow, stood puzzling and puzzling, how could it be so? It came without ribbons. It came without tags. It came without packages, boxes or bags. And he puzzled and puzzled 'till his puzzler was sore.

"Then the Grinch thought of something he hadn't before. What if Christmas, he thought, doesn't come from a store. What if Christmas, perhaps, means a little bit more." *- Dr. Seuss (1904 – 1991) "How the Grinch Stole Christmas!"*

Holiday Toast: "During these Holidays, may you always keep your friends close, your enemies closer, and receipts for all major purchases." *- Bridger Winegar, Writer and Actor*

Charles Halloran: "All right, you go back and tell them that the New York State Supreme Court rules there's no Santa Claus. It's all over the papers. The kids read it and they don't hang up their stockings. Now what happens to all the toys that are supposed to be in those stockings? Nobody buys them. The toy manufacturers are not going to like that; so, they have to lay off a lot of their employees, union employees. Now you got the CIO and the AF of L against ya and they're going to adore ya for it and they're going to say it with votes. Oh, and the department stores are going to love ya too and the Christmas card makers and the candy companies. Ho ho, Henry, you're going to be an awful popular fella. And what about the

Salvation Army? Why, they got a Santy Claus on every corner, and they're taking a fortune…

"But you go ahead Henry, you do it your way. You go on back in there and tell them that you rule there is no Santy Claus. Go on. But if you do, remember this: you can count on getting just two votes, your own and that district attorney's out there."

Judge Henry X. Harper: [shaking his head No] "The DA's a Republican." *- From the movie "Miracle on 34th Street"*

"My beerdrunk soul is sadder than all the dead Christmas trees of the world." *- Charles Bukowski, (1920 – 1994) Poet, Novelist, and Short Story Writer*

"CALVIN said, 'This whole Santa Claus thing just doesn't make sense. Why all the secrecy? Why all the mystery? If the guy exists why doesn't he ever show himself and prove it? And if he doesn't exist what's the meaning of all this?'"

HOBBES replied, "I dunno. Isn't this a religious holiday?"

CALVIN: 'Yeah, but actually, I've got the same questions about God.'" *- Bill Watterson, author of syndicated comic strip Calvin and Hobbes*

"My idea of Christmas, whether old-fashioned or modern, is very simple: loving others. Come to think of it, why do we have to wait for Christmas to do that?" *- Bob Hope*

"The Supreme Court has ruled that they cannot have a nativity scene in Washington, D.C. This wasn't for any religious reasons. They couldn't find three wise men and a virgin." *- Jay Leno, American comedian, actor, writer, producer, and television host.*

"Christmas can be celebrated in the school room with pine trees, tinsel and reindeers, but there must be no mention of the man whose birthday is being celebrated. One wonders how a teacher would answer if a student asked why it was called Christmas." *- Ronald Reagan (1911 - 2004) 40th President of the United States*

"This holiday season, no matter what your religion is, please take a moment to reflect on

why it's better than all the other ones." *- Guy Endore Kaiser, Author*

"Christmas is doing a little something extra for someone." *- Charles M. Schulz (1922 – 2000) Syndicated comic strip "Peanuts"*

Fred Gailey: "Your Honor, every one of these letters is addressed to Santa Claus. The Post Office has delivered them. Therefore, the Post Office Department, a branch of the Federal Government, recognizes this man Kris Kringle to be the one and only Santa Claus."

Judge Henry X. Harper: "Uh, since the United States Government declares this man to be Santa Claus, this court will not dispute it. Case dismissed." *- From the movie "Miracle on 34th Street"*

"The worst gift is a fruitcake. There is only one fruitcake in the entire world, and people keep sending it to each other." *- Johnny Carson (1925 – 2005), Comedian and TV Host*

"It's harder to talk about, but what I really, really, really want for Christmas is just this: I want to be 5 years old again for an hour. I want to laugh a lot and cry a lot. I want to be picked or rocked to sleep in someone's arms and carried up to be just one more time. I know what I really want for Christmas: I want my childhood back. People who think good thoughts give good gifts." *- Robert Fulghum, Author, "All I Really Need to Know I Learned in Kindergarten"*

Clark Griswold: "Hey! If any of you are looking for any last-minute gift ideas for me, I have one.

"I'd like Frank Shirley, my boss, right here tonight. I want him brought from his happy holiday slumber over there on Melody Lane with all the other rich people and I want him brought right here, with a big ribbon on his head, and I want to look him straight in the eye and I want to tell him what a cheap, lying, no-good, rotten, four-flushing, low-life, snake-licking, dirt-eating, inbred, overstuffed, ignorant, blood-sucking, dog-kissing, brainless, dickless, hopeless, heartless, fat-ass, bug-eyed, stiff-legged, spotty-lipped, worm-headed sack of monkey sh*t he is! Hallelujah! Holy shit! Where's the Tylenol?" *- National Lampoon's Christmas Vacation (1989)*

Holiday Toast: "Christmas is here again. Let us raise a loving cup; Peace on earth, goodwill to men, and make them do the washing up." - *Wendy Cope*

"It's for the hamster that I'm gonna buy! This is so perfect!" (after opening a hamster wheel at Christmas)" - *Gerard Way, American singer, songwriter, musician, and comic book writer*

"I never believed in Santa Claus. None of us kids did. Mom and Dad refused to let us. They couldn't afford expensive presents and they didn't want us to think we weren't as good as other kids who, on Christmas morning, found all sorts of fancy toys under the tree that were supposedly left by Santa Claus.

Dad had lost his job at the gypsum, and when Christmas came that year, we had no money at all. On Christmas Eve, Dad took each one of us kids out into the desert night one by one.

'Pick out your favorite star', Dad said.

'I like that one!' I said.

Dad grinned, 'that's Venus', he said. He explained to me that planets glowed because reflected light was constant, and stars twinkled because their light pulsed.

'I like it anyway,' I said.

'What the hell,' Dad said. 'It's Christmas. You can have a planet if you want.'

And he gave me Venus…

We laughed about all the kids who believed in the Santa myth and got nothing for Christmas but a bunch of cheap plastic toys. 'Years from now, when all the junk they got is broken and long forgotten,' Dad said, 'you'll still have your stars.' *- Jeannette Walls, Author of "The Glass Castle"*

"Love the giver more than the gift." *- Brigham Young (1801 – 1877), Religious leader, politician, and settler*

"A good time; a kind, forgiving, charitable, pleasant time: the only time I know of, in the long calendar of the year, when men and women seem by one consent to open their shut-up hearts freely." *- Charles Dickens*

"Peace on earth

Will come to stay,

When we live

Christmas every day."

- Helen Steiner Rice (1900 – 1981) American writer of religious and inspirational poetry

"Just before Christmas, an honest politician, a generous lawyer and Santa Claus all got into the lift of the hotel.

As the lift traveled from the 5th floor down to the ground level, one-by-one they noticed a large roll of $100 bills was lying on the lift's floor.

Which one of them picked up the roll of hundreds and handed it in at reception?

Santa of course, the other two don't actually exist!" *- Christmas-day.org*

"Once again, we find ourselves enmeshed in the Holiday Season, that very special time of year when we join with our loved ones in

sharing centuries-old traditions such as trying to find a parking space at the mall. We traditionally do this in my family by driving around the parking lot until we see a shopper emerge from the mall, then we follow her, in very much the same spirit as the Three Wise Men, who 2,000 years ago followed a star, week after week, until it led them to a parking space."
- Dave Barry, American author and columnist

"Christmas will always be as long as we stand heart to heart and hand in hand." *- Dr. Seuss*

"The best of all gifts around any Christmas tree: the presence of a happy family all wrapped up in each other." *- Burton Hills (1883 – 1963) Member of the House of Commons of Canada*

Holiday Toast: "Here's to the good old days when people would stop Christmas shopping when they ran out of money." *- Anon*

"There I am, watching Philip Seymour Hoffman, one of my favourite actors in the world, walk into the room dressed up as Father Christmas,

being hilarious, and I'm suddenly thinking, where am I?" *- Tom Sturridge, English actor*

"At Christmas, it's my siblings running around the house, we're cooking, talking, laughing, loud and just crazy. It's beautiful chaos." *- Tika Sumpter, American actress, producer, television host, and model*

"I was supposed to be working on 'The Weekenders,' but I was blocked. I got this crazy idea that I would make Christmas stockings out of blankets." *- Mary Kay Andrews, NY Times Bestselling Author*

Holiday Toast: "Here's a Holiday wish to all. May you never forget what is worth remembering or remember what is best forgotten." *- Anon*

"It's not exactly calm at Christmas. It's a bit like the Simpsons appearing in a pasta advert - lots of bickering, crazy pets, and plenty of tomato sauce!" *- Sophia Di Martino, British Actress*

"Gifts of time and love are surely the basic ingredients of a truly merry Christmas." *- Peg Bracken, (1918 – 2007) American author and humorist*

"And in despair I bowed my head;

'There is no peace on earth,' I said;

'For hate is strong,

And mocks the song

Of peace on earth, good-will to men!'"

Then pealed the bells more loud and deep:

'God is not dead, nor doth he sleep!

The Wrong shall fail,

the Right prevail,

With peace on earth, good-will to men!'"

- Henry Wadsworth Longfellow (1807 – 1882), American poet and educator

"I got stoned crazy when I saw somebody run down them strings with a bottleneck. My eyes lit up like a Christmas tree and I said that I had to

learn." - *Muddy Waters (1913 – 1983) American blues singer-songwriter and musician*

"One good thing about Christmas shopping is it toughens you for the January sales." - *Grace Kriley*

"He who has not Christmas in his heart will not find it under the tree." - *Roy L. Smith (1887 – 1963) American Clergyman*

George Bailey: "Just a minute... just a minute. Now, hold on, Mr. Potter. You're right when you say my father was no businessman. I know that. Why he ever started this cheap, penny-ante Building and Loan, I'll never know.

"But neither you nor anyone else can say anything against his character, because his whole life was... why, in the 25 years since he and his brother, Uncle Billy, started this thing, he never once thought of himself. Isn't that right, Uncle Billy?

"My father didn't save enough money to send Harry away to college, let alone me. But he did help a few people get out of your slums, Mr. Potter, and what's wrong with that?

"Why... here, you're all businessmen here. Doesn't it make them better citizens? Doesn't it make them better customers? You... you said... what'd you say a minute ago, 'They had to wait and save their money before they even ought to think of a decent home?' Wait? Wait for what? Until their children grow up and leave them? Until they're so old and broken down that they...Do you know how long it takes a working man to save $5,000?

"Just remember this, Mr. Potter, that this rabble you're talking about... they do most of the working and paying and living and dying in this community. Well, is it too much to have them work and pay and live and die in a couple of decent rooms and a bath?

"Anyway, my father didn't think so. People were human beings to him. But to you, a warped, frustrated old man, they're cattle. Well in my book, my father died a much richer man than you'll ever be!" *- From the movie, "It's a Wonderful Life"*

Holiday Toast: "Here's to Peace on Earth, Goodwill to Men, and having batteries when they're not included." *- Anon*

"When you spend such a large portion of your life working - and it's not fun, and you're worried about getting sued or fired for saying the wrong thing or for acting crazy at a work party - then what has work done to America? That's the impetus to have a huge office Christmas party." *- T. J. Miller, American actor, stand-up comedian, producer, and writer*

"What I don't like about office Christmas parties is looking for a job the next day." *- Phyllis Diller, American comedian*

"You can mess with a lot of things, but you can't mess with kids on Christmas." *- From the movie, "Home Alone 2"*

"Ever wonder what people got Jesus for Christmas? It's like, "Oh great, socks. You know I'm dying for your sins, right? Yeah, but thanks for the socks! They'll go great with my sandals. What am I, German?" *- Jim Gaffigan, American comedian*

Holiday Toast: "Men are not the equal of women. Just look at a man trying to wrap a

Christmas present. Men, raise a glass and here's to wrapping all your Christmas presents well, at least make it look like the gift put up a good fight. *" - Anon*

"Christmas is not as much about opening presents as opening our hearts." *- J.L.W. Brooks, American movie producer, director and screenwriter*

"Christmas to a child is the first terrible proof that to travel hopefully is better than to arrive." *- Stephen Fry, English comedian, actor, writer, and presenter*

"The milk and cookies are still here but the presents are all gone! I've been robbed by a diabetic!" *- Albert Brooks, American actor, comedian, writer, and director*

"Time cannot be packaged and ribboned and left under trees for Christmas morning. Time can't be given. But it can be shared" *- Cecelia Ahern, Author of "The Gift"*

"Do what you do. This Christmas, Hanukkah, Kwanzaa, New Year's Eve, Twelfth Night, Valentine's Day, Mardi Gras, St. Paddy's Day, and every day henceforth. Just do what you do. Live out your life and your traditions on your own terms.

"If it offends others, so be it. That's their problem." *- Chris Rose, New York Times Best-Selling writer and journalist.*

"I planned out our whole day: First, we'll make snow angels for two hours, and then we'll go ice skating, and then we'll eat a whole roll of Toll-House cookie dough as fast as we can, and then to finish, we'll snuggle." *- From the movie, "Elf"*

"Let's just say that on this day, a million years ago, a dude was born who most of us think was magic. But others don't, and that's cool. But we're probably right. Amen." *- Homer Simpson*

"Christmas Eve was a night of song that wrapped itself about you like a shawl. But it warmed more than your body. It warmed your heart...filled it, too, with melody that would last

forever.” *- Bess Streeter Aldrich (1881 - 1954), American Author, "Song of Years"*

"You know you're getting old, when Santa starts looking younger." *-Bart Simpson, The Simpsons: Miracle on Evergreen Terrace*

"See, the thing is I didn't think that that song would get much attention because it's such a personal song to me. I just wrote it about my childhood, and I didn't know how that would read on an album.

"But it's been everybody's favorite song. I didn't tell my mom. It was a total secret. So, I wrote it in secret and then decided to record it secretly, so she had no idea that the song was recorded.

"My producers sent me the track and I synched it up to all my baby videos and I played it for her one Christmas Eve, and she bawled her eyes out. She didn't even think that it was my song. She didn't think there was any way for me to record a song without her knowing." *- Taylor Swift, on her song "The Best Day"*

"I hate Christmas. The mall is full of nothing but women and children. All you hear is, 'I want

this,' 'Get me this,' 'I have to have this'… and then there's the children. And they're all by my store 'cause they stuck the mall Santa right outside ringing his stupid bell. As if you need a bell to notice a 300-pound alcoholic in a red suit. 'Ho, ho, ho,' all day long. So, nice as can be, I go outside, ask him to shut the hell up. He takes a swing at me. So, I lay a hook into his fat belly and he goes down. Beard comes off, all the kids start crying and I'm the bad guy." *- Al Bundy in Married with Children*

Holiday Toast: "Here's to the warmth of home and hearth, the cheer and good will of friends, and the hope of a childlike heart to you all." - A toast from An O'Brien Family Christmas

"Our hearts grow tender with childhood memories and love of kindred, and we are better throughout the year for having, in spirit, become a child again at Christmas-time." - *Laura Ingalls Wilder (1867 – 1957), American writer best known for her "Little House on the Prairie series"*

"Unless we make Christmas an occasion to share our blessings, all the snow in Alaska won't make it white." *- Bing Crosby (1903 – 1977), American singer and actor*

"If I were Satan, I'd make the symbol of Easter an egg, and the symbol of Christmas, a bottle.

"If I were the devil, I would take from those who have, and I would give to those who wanted, until I had killed the incentive of the ambitious.

"And then, my police state would force everybody back to work. Then, I could separate families, putting children in uniform, women in coal mines, and objectors in slave camps.

"In other words, if I were Satan, I'd just keep on doing what he's doing." *- Paul Harvey, Radio commentator from a speech broadcast on ABC Radio on April 3, 1965*

"Let the children have their night of fun and laughter.

"Let the gifts of Father Christmas delight their play.

"Let us grown-ups share to the full in their unstinted pleasures before we turn again to the

stern task and the formidable years that lie before us, resolved that, by our sacrifice and daring, these same children shall not be robbed of their inheritance or denied their right to live in a free and decent world." *- Winston Churchill (1874 – 1965) Christmas Eve Message, 1941*

"Christmas is a time when you get homesick – even when you're home." *- Carol Nelson, Author*

"Ma!" she cried. "There is a Santa Claus, isn't there?"

"Of course, there's a Santa Claus," said Ma.

"The older you are, the more you know about Santa Claus," she said. "You are so big now, you know he can't be just one man, don't you? You know he is everywhere on Christmas Eve. He is in the Big Woods, and in Indian Territory, and far away in York State, and here. He comes down all the chimneys at the same time. You know that, don't you?"

"Yes, Ma," said Mary and Laura.

"Well," said Ma. "Then you see--"

"I guess he is like angels," Mary said, slowly. And Laura could see that, just as well as Mary could.

"Then Ma told them something else about Santa Claus. He was everywhere, and besides that, he was all the time. Whenever anyone was unselfish, that was Santa Claus. Christmas Eve was the time when everybody was unselfish. On that one night, Santa Claus was everywhere, because everybody, all together, stopped being selfish and wanted other people to be happy. And in the morning, you saw what that had done.

"If everybody wanted everybody else to be happy all the time, then would it be Christmas all the time?" Laura asked, and Ma said, "Yes, Laura." - Laura Ingalls Wilder (1867 – 1957) American author

"One of the most glorious messes in the world is the mess created in the living room on Christmas day. Don't clean it up too quickly." - *J. L. W. Brooks, American director, producer and screenwriter*

"Never worry about the size of your Christmas tree. In the eyes of all children, it's 30 feet tall." *- Larry Wilde, Comedian*

Holiday Toast: "Here's to the year past and friends who have left us. Here's to the present and the friends who are here. Here's to the Holidays and the New Year and the new friends who will join us." *- Emily Post*

"Nothing says holidays like a cheese log." *- Ellen DeGeneres*

"I throw a Christmas party at my house. It's not really a Christmas party, because I don't want to call it a Christmas party. But let's just say I put a lot of Christmas trees around the house, so it smells good." *- Bill Murray, Comedian*

Clark Griswold: "Where do you think you're going? Nobody's leaving. Nobody's walking out on this fun, old-fashioned family Christmas.

"No, no. We're all in this together. This is a full-blown, four-alarm holiday emergency here.

"We're gonna press on, and we're gonna have the hap, hap, happiest Christmas since Bing Crosby tap-danced with Danny f*cking Kaye. And when Santa squeezes his fat white ass down that chimney tonight, he's gonna find the jolliest bunch of assh*les this side of the nuthouse." *- National Lampoon's Christmas Vacation (1989)*

Holiday Toast: "Wishing you more happiness than all my words can tell, not just for the holidays, but for all the year as well." *- Anon*

Charlie Brown: "I guess you were right, Linus. I shouldn't have picked this little tree. Everything I do turns into a disaster. I guess I really don't know what Christmas is all about.

[shouting in desperation]

Charlie Brown: "Isn't there anyone who knows what Christmas is all about?"

Linus Van Pelt: "Sure, Charlie Brown, I can tell you what Christmas is all about."

[moves toward the center of the stage]

Linus Van Pelt: "Lights, please."

[a spotlight shines on Linus]

Linus Van Pelt: "And there were in the same country shepherds abiding in the field, keeping watch over their flock by night. And lo, the angel of the Lord came upon them, and the glory of the Lord shone round about them: and they were sore afraid. And the angel said unto them, 'Fear not'

[Linus drops his security blanket on purpose]

Linus Van Pelt: 'for behold, I bring unto you good tidings of great joy, which shall be to all people. For unto you is born this day in the City of David a Savior, which is Christ the Lord. And this shall be a sign unto you; Ye shall find the babe wrapped in swaddling clothes, lying in a manger.' And suddenly there was with the angel a multitude of the heavenly host, praising God, and saying, 'Glory to God in the highest, and on earth peace, good will toward men.'" [Luke 2:8-14 KJV]

Linus Van Pelt: [Linus picks up his blanket and walks back towards Charlie Brown] "That's what Christmas is all about, Charlie Brown." - *From "A Charlie Brown Christmas"*

New Year Quotes & Toasts

"The more specific you are about your resolution, the better your chance of sticking with it. Don't just say, 'I want to lose weight.' Say, 'When my arm jiggles, I want it to look less like a pelican's throat-pouch choking down a bass.'" *- Colin Nissan*

"Past and Present I know well; each is a friend and sometimes an enemy to me. But it is the quiet, beckoning future of a New Year, an absolute stranger, with whom I have fallen madly in love." *- Richelle E. Goodrich, Author, "Slaying Dragons"*

"Hope smiles from the threshold of the year to come,

Whispering 'it will be happier'..." *- Alfred Lord Tennyson (1809 – 1892) Poet Laureate of Great Britain and Ireland*

"My New Year's resolution is to spend less time interacting with people and more time on my phone. It is working very well so far…" *- Anon.*

New Year Toast: "May the New Year make any pain you have make you stronger. May your tears make you braver. May heartbreaks make you wiser. And may vodka make you not remember any of that crap." *- Anon*

"In fact, my New Year's resolution every year, (and I'm Jewish so I get two New Years a year) is to meditate, and I fail every time." *- Sheryl Sandberg, American technology executive, activist, author, and billionaire.*

"The object of a New Year is not that we should have a new year. It is that we should have a new soul and a new nose; new feet, a new backbone, new ears, and new eyes. Unless a particular man made New Year resolutions, he would make no resolutions. Unless a man starts

afresh about things, he will certainly do nothing effective." - G. K. Chesterton (1874 – 1936) English writer, poet, and philosopher

"I don't believe in New Year's resolutions. I think if you want to change something, change it today and don't wait until the New Year." - *Georgina Bloomberg, American philanthropist and professional equestrian*

Bill O'Reilly's questioned the grammar of "Happy Holidays" and Jon Stewart responded: "Christmas and the New Year are actually two holidays. So, there is a plural, which in the English language, necessitates the use of 's.' I suppose you could say 'Merry Christmas' and 'Happy New Year,' but you probably have sh*t to do." *- Jon Stewart, American comedian*

"The proper behavior all through the holiday season is to be drunk. This drunkenness culminates on New Year's Eve, when you get so drunk you kiss the person you're married to." - *P.J. O'Rourke, American political satirist*

"New Year's Resolution: To tolerate fools more gladly, provided this does not encourage them to take up more of my time." *- James Agate (1877 – 1947) English diarist and theatre critic*

New Year Toast: "Here's to always forgiving your enemies; nothing annoys them so much." *- Oscar Wilde*

"New Year's Resolution #17: To become as fat as I was the very first time I thought I was fat." *- Kenzie Fei*

"Now there are more overweight people in America than average-weight people. So, overweight people are now average and your resolve to try and be average weight, well, you've met your New Year's resolution." *- Jay Leno, Comedian*

"Work on your strengths, not your weaknesses. How many of your New Year's resolutions have been about fixing a flaw? And how many of those resolutions have you made several years in a row? It's difficult to change any aspect of your personality by sheer force of will, and if it is a weakness you choose to work on, you probably won't enjoy the process. If you don't find pleasure or reinforcement along the way, then—unless you have the willpower of Ben Franklin—you'll soon give up.

"But you don't really have to be good at everything. Life offers so many chances to use one tool instead of another, and often you can use a strength to get around a weakness." - *Jonathan Haidt, Author of "The Happiness Hypothesis: Finding Modern Truth in Ancient Wisdom"*

New Year Toast: "May your pants always smell fresh in the New Year when you pick them up each morning, so you can wear them the next day." - *Anon*

"Live a life abundant in love and rich in spirit, these are the seeds of a fulfilling existence. Be the safe harbor you seek in the world. Follow your dreams, not your fear.

"Go into the New Year with an open mind and hopeful heart. Don't let the chains of unforgiveness weigh you down. Life is too short to live in a prison of past hurts. The future is yours for the taking and creating.

"Life is bittersweet, when we can let darkness and light co-exist as illumination, we can live in true happiness. When we live life at its best, it is a symphony of feelings, of high and low notes, of tragedy and comedy, love and loss, magic and the sublime. It can be quite a spectacular journey when we fully embrace and accept it." - *Jaeda DeWalt, Author of "Chasing Desdemona"*

New Year Toast: "Let us have wine and women, mirth and laughter, and sermons and soda-water the day after." - *Lord Byron (1788 – 1824) British nobleman, poet, and politician*

"My New Year's Eve is always 2 July, the night before my birthday. That's the night I make my resolutions. And this year scares the life out of me, because no matter how successful, how good things appear, there is always a deep core of failure within me, although I am trying to deal with it. My biggest fear, this coming year, is that I will be waking up alone.

"It makes me wonder how many bodies will be fished out of the Thames, how many decaying corpses will be found in one-room flats.

"I'm just being realistic." *- Tracey Emin, "Strangeland"*

"A New Year's resolution is something that goes in one year and out the other." *- Anon*

"As we did every New Year's Eve, we made ridiculous resolutions that no one would keep, and quietly we all wondered what the coming year would hold, each of us praying for our own private miracles. Good health. Better health. A marriage for this child, a good job for another. This hopefulness was something hardwired into

our psyches, that a new year might mean some monumental something wonderful could happen to bring us happiness at a level we had never known. A new year was a chance to start over. Maybe even, just maybe, there would be peace on earth for one entire day." - *Dorothea Benton Frank, The Last Original Wife*

New Year Toast: "Here's to a long life and a merry one. A quick death and an easy one. A pretty girl and an honest one. A cold beer - and another one!" - *Anon*

MOTHER TIME: "Life goes by so very fast, my dears, and taking the time to reflect, even once a year, slows things down. We zoom past so many seconds, minutes, hours, killing them with the frantic way we live that it's important we take at least this one collective sigh and stop, take stock, and acknowledge our place in time before diving back into the melee. Midnight on New Year's Eve is a unique kind of magic where, just for a moment, the past and the future exist at once in the present. Whether we're aware of it or not, as we countdown

together to it, we're sharing the burden of our history and committing to the promise of tomorrow." *- Hillary DePiano, New Year's Thieve*

"There is nothing magical about the flip of the calendar, but it represents a clean break, a new hope, and a blank canvas." *- Jason Soroski, American singer and songwriter*

"Each year's regrets are envelopes in which messages of hope are found for the New Year." *- John R. Dallas Jr., "We Need to Have a Word: Words of Wisdom, Courage and Patience for Work, Home and Everywhere"*

New Year Toast: "May your neighbors respect you, trouble neglect you, the angels protect you, and heaven accept you." *- Anon*

"The only way to spend New Year's Eve is either quietly with friends or in a brothel. Otherwise when the evening ends and people

pair off, someone is bound to be left in tears.” - W.H. Auden (1907 – 1973) English-American poet

New Year Toast: **“Here's health to those I love and wealth to those who love me.”** - *Anon*

“It seems silly to worry about the arbitrary moment some person long dead declared to be the end of one year and the beginning of another, as if our attempts to divide time into meaningful chunks actually mean anything. People wait for the countdown to tell them it's okay to believe in themselves again. They end each year with failure, but hope that when the clock strikes twelve, they can begin the new year with a clean slate. They tell themselves that this is the year things will happen, never realizing that things are always happening; they're just happening without them.” - *Shaun David Hutchinson, Author “We Are the Ants”*

“A New Year's resolution that I can never keep? To be able to make decisions.” - *Ashanti,*

American singer, songwriter, record producer, dancer and actress

"If you asked me for my New Year Resolution, it would be to find out who I am." - Cyril Cusack (1910 – 1993), Irish actor

"New Year's resolutions work like this: you think of something you enjoy doing and then resolve to stop doing it." *- Charlie Brooker, English humourist, author, screenwriter, and producer*

New Year Toast: "Here's to alcohol: the cause of, and solution to, all of life's problems." *- Homer Simpson*

"I have no way of knowing how people really feel, but the vast majority of those I meet couldn't be nicer. Every once in a while someone barks at me. My New Year's resolution

is not to bark back.” *- Tucker Carlson, American commentator*

“Dieting on New Year's Day isn't a good idea as you can't eat rationally but really need to be free to consume whatever is necessary, moment by moment, in order to ease your hangover. I think it would be much more sensible if resolutions began generally on January the second.” - *Helen Fielding, English author*

“My New Year’s resolution is not to eat chocolate on the days ending in ‘y’” *- Anon*

“If you decide to cut something out this year, try replacing it with something else to balance out the loss. If you stop drinking soda, for example, replace it with becoming more sedentary. You deserve it. You loved soda. *” - Colin Nissan*

"You can never make this New Year as your best year because your best year is always the year you were born! When the fireworks start, be thankful for your existence and for everything which made this possible!" - Mehmet Murat ildan, Turkish playwright and novelist

"Oy, Jake," he said, shaking his head, like a benevolent rabbi I'd disappointed with my weak will. "Impatience. Seriously. I know this is hard for you …" He glazed over. Drifted a moment. Went through something in his impenetrable interior … "Actually, I do know this is hard for you. I'm sorry. I'm not using my imagination- that was my New Year's resolution, you know. Work on standing in the other fellow's shoes. That and to read one poem every day." *- Glen Duncan, Author, "The Last Werewolf"*

"I don't believe in New Year Resolutions. I believe in new day or new hour resolutions." *- Robert Braathe, Educator*

"Happiness is too many things these days for anyone to wish it on anyone lightly. So, let's just wish each other a bile/less New Year and leave it at that." *- Judith Crist, American film critic*

"The past is always tense, the future perfect." *- Zadie Smith, British Novelist*

"Underneath my grief that day a resolution was hardening into cement: I would never, ever again create something thinking that I would be able to preserve it." *- Marcia Tucker, Author, "A Short Life of Trouble: Forty Years in the New York Art World"*

"I don't have a New Year's resolution. You don't need them when you're perfect." *– Anon*

"I muttered a swear word to myself. After I heard Angel cussing like a sailor when she

stubbed her toe, my new resolution was to watch my language. All I needed was a six-year-old mutant with a potty mouth" *- James Patterson, Author, from "The Angel Experiment"*

"On New Year's Eve the whole world celebrates the fact that a date changes. Let us celebrate the dates on which we change the world." - Akilnathan Logeswaran, German activist for Human Rights

"People would cheer throw confetti and then go about breaking the resolutions they had made only moments before." *- Neal Shusterman, NY Times bestselling author, from his book "Downsiders"*

New Year Toast: "May you always do sober what you said you'd do drunk and that will teach you to keep your mouth shut." *- Ernest Hemingway*

"The whole point to New Years is not just to have a new year. But that we should be new, better and different people. That is why we exercise to RE-NEW our bodies. That is why we write GOALS to get a Renewed sense of our potential. That is why we make RE-SOLUTIONS because we resolve that there are solutions inside of us that we have not tapped into. So, don't waste each New Year's season. Maximize it! Start fresh using a new perspective for it will enable you to tap into a new season with greater capacity." *- Stella Payton, Author*

Resolution: "I will not cling to my boyfriend next year like a colony of E. Coli and he was room-temperature Canadian beef." *– Anon*

New Year Toast: "May your troubles be less, and your blessings be more. And nothing but happiness come through your door." *- Anon*

"This is the new year the new you. You can pass through another year, coasting on cruise control. Or you can step out of your comfort

zone, trying things you have never done before, & make 2012 (or any other year) as the year that you elevate from where you are & soar high. Make it happen!" - Pablo, Author

"People are so worried about what they eat between Christmas and the New Year, but they really should be worried about what they eat between the New Year and Christmas." - *Anon*

"It's suspended there (the Ball in Times Square) to remind us before we pop the champagne and celebrate the New Year, to stop and reflect on the year that has gone by.

"To remember both our triumphs and our missteps - our promises made and broken.

"The times we opened ourselves up to great adventures - or closed ourselves down, for fear of getting hurt. Because that's what New Year's is all about: getting another chance. A chance to forgive, to do better, to do more, to give more, to love more. And stop worrying about 'what if' and start embracing what would be. So, when that ball drops at midnight - and it will

drop - let's remember to be nice to each other, kind to each other. And not just tonight but all year long." *- Claire Morgan, from the movie "New Year's Eve, Warner Brothers*

"An optimist stays up until midnight to see the new year in. A pessimist stays up to make sure the old year leaves." *- Bill Vaughn (1915 – 1977), American columnist and author*

"Cheers to a new year and another chance for us to get it right." *- Oprah Winfrey*

"New Year's Day: Now is the accepted time to make your regular annual good resolutions. Next week you can begin paving hell with them as usual." *- Mark Twain*

New Year Toast: "In the new year, may your right hand always be stretched out in friendship, but never in want." *- Anon*

"On the night of New Year's Day, I thought of a wonderful New Year's resolution for the men who run the world: get to know the people who only live in it." - Martha Gellhorn, Author, from "The Face of War"

"This year has taught me the simple craft of belief. I believe in the things I've nurtured and built this year. Slowly but carefully. Such as understanding, knowledge, passion, strength; the hundreds of songs I've written, the 365 poems, the books I've read and the miles I've run. The resolution to breathe, to meditate, to not harm my mind or body even when I've felt like it." - Charlotte Eriksson, Author and songwriter

"Many years ago, I made a New Year's resolution to never make New Year's resolutions. Hell, it's been the only resolution I've ever kept!" - *D.S. Mixell, Author*

"I am grateful for all that this year has given me, including the lessons it has given to my soul.

This year I will be kinder and more compassionate to myself and to all beings.

I will stop being so hard on me.

I will laugh more.

I will unplug more.

I will shift into my heart more.

I will make the time to connect to the Divine and feed my spirit.

I will let go of the small stuff.

I will surround myself with uplifting people and activities.

This is my truth and so it is. Amen." *- Eileen Anglin, Life Coach, Writer, Artist and Activist*

"My New Year's Resolution List usually starts with the desire to lose between ten and three thousand pounds." *- Nia Vardalos, Canadian-American actress, screenwriter, and producer*

New Year Toast: "May the best day of your past be the worst day of your future." *- Anon*

"I believe in living life the way that you want to live it every day, and if you do that, you don't really need to have New Year's resolutions." - Tom Ford, American fashion designer

Thank you very much for reading our book and if you liked it, we would appreciate your leaving a short review on Amazon.

We love to hear your thoughts and suggestions on anything and please feel free to contact us at TeamGolfwell@gmail.com. And have a great Holiday Season and a wonderful New Year!

www.TeamGolfwell.com

Team Golfwell's Other Books

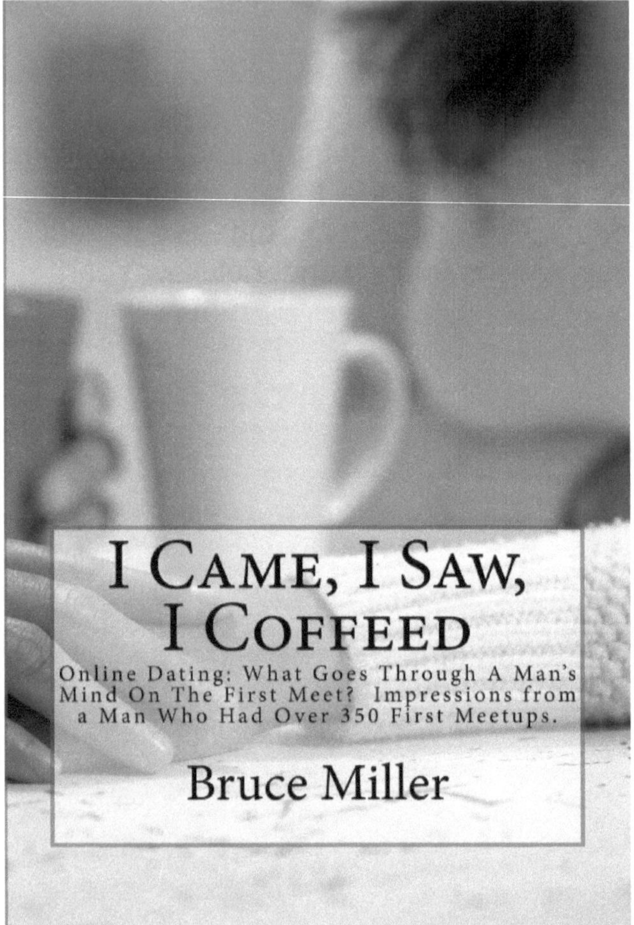

Why Didn't He Call Me Back? Impressions From a Man Who Had Over 350 First Meetups

Team Golfwell's Other Books

Walk the Winning Ways of Golf's Greatests

For Young Golfers, Junior Golfers, First Tee

Team Golfwell's Other Books

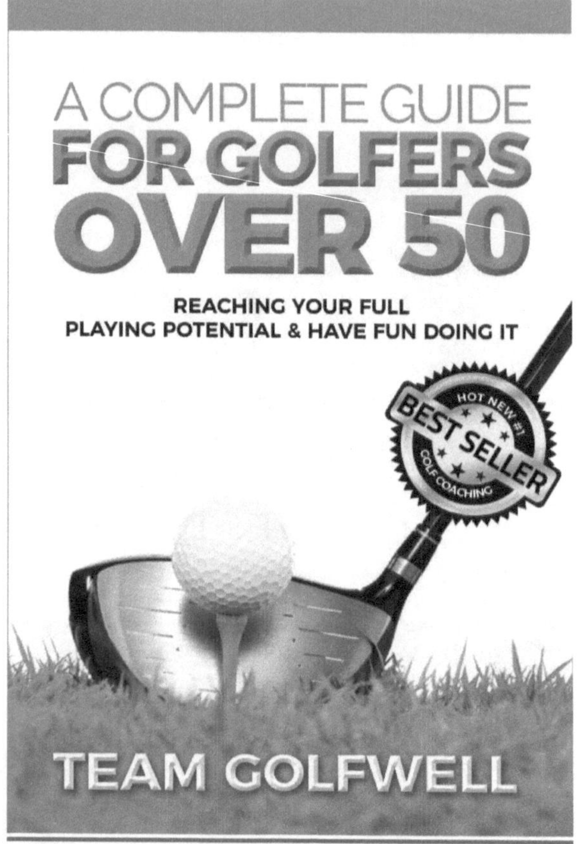

A Complete Guide For Golfers Over 50: Reaching Your Full Playing Potential & Have Fun Doing It. (Over 300 pages)